Poena Damni

With the people from the bridge

By the same author:

Poena Damni, Z213: Exit. Translated by Shorsha Sullivan.
Shoestring Press, Nottingham 2010.

Poena Damni, The First Death. Translated by Shorsha Sullivan.
Shoestring Press, Nottingham 2000.

Printed by Imprint Digital
Upton Pyne, Exeter, Devon EX5 5HY
info@imprintdigital.com

Published by Shoestring Press
19 Devonshire Avenue,
Beeston, Nottingham NG9 1BS
tel: +44(0115) 925 1827 e: info@shoestringpress.com

First published in English: 2014
Copyright: Dimitris Lyacos and Shorsha Sullivan 2014
ISBN 978-1-910323-15-1
Title of the original: ΜΕ ΤΟΥΣ ΑΝΘΡΩΠΟΥΣ
ΑΠΟ ΤΗ ΓΕΦΥΡΑ

Artwork for the present edition: Gudrun Bielz
Cover design, layout: Nassos Dimakis

DIMITRIS LYACOS

With the people from the bridge

Translated by Shorsha Sullivan

With the people from the bridge

for Vassilis,

Night had already fallen when I crossed to the other side of the station and came out on to the road. It was still raining, a little. I would find them in one of the arches under the bridge, as he had told me. I would see light. I arrived outside, I waited. We waited. They opened. We entered. We were given a handout. Inside you could see up to a point, then dark. I sat on the dirt floor among the others, ten, more or less, some of them with their dogs. On the left the wall crumbling. Two more coming from there. Three. Lights, high up opposite blue, green on the right and white lamps hanging, five or six, from the ceiling exactly above us, lit except one. On one side the women. Three around a cut-down oil drum, another one fetching newspapers. They tore some up and threw them inside. Fire. It went out. Again. When they moved back for a moment, close to the wall, you could hardly discern them, was it their clothes or the light that was making it look like that. And they kept opening and closing their eyes all the time, like spasms reaching as far as their mouth - apart from the one on the left that was probably younger. Now this man, passing them naked to the waist with a broken brick or stone? in his hand and coming our way. A scar like a word on his chest, from his neck downwards. Sits down, takes two pieces of wood, hammers, he made a cross. Sticks it in the mud. To the side a glass and a bottle. Further back, the shell of a car half-buried, front door missing. On the bonnet a cassette-player and a television, the wind-screen covered by a sheet

With the people from the bridge // 11

of iron. A woman comes out from the car. It had seemed empty a few moments ago, you wouldn't have known she was there. From her nose down, like a mask made of earth, mouth hardly visible. Goes inside again, pulls a wooden cover in front. Drags it shut but can't altogether do it. Old bits of iron around. Engine-parts. And another man walking about, coming to us. Haggard, torn pullover, book in hand, some papers inside. Four names on the handout they gave me: Narrator – the one holding the book. Like a Bible. Turns the cassette-player on and off. Hum. Goes and helps the women. More newspapers, Chorus – the women. LG – further back, he was hammering something again. NCTV – her in the car. LG, NCTV. These were the names. Title: NCTV. That is how I remember the name of the station, vaguely somehow. Nyctovo. No. Nyctivo. Nichtovo. No. Another hum, louder, going on from the time I came in. Cassette-player. Narrator. Turns on and off, goes away, comes again opens the Bible, tears pages from there and goes and glues them on the wall to the right, one beside the other. Then he waits. He waits. With his back turned, almost. On one side and on the other crosses sprayed on the concrete. He comes here to read. Narrator. Lights above turned out.

> And always, night
> and day in the tombs
> and in the mountains he was crying
> and cutting himself with stones.

But when he saw Jesus afar
off he ran
and worshipped him,
and cried with a loud voice,
and said; what have I to do with you, Jesus,
son of the most high God?
I adjure thee by God,
that thou torment me not.
For he said unto him; come out thou
unclean spirit from the
man, and he asked him;
what is thy name? and he answered
saying; my name is legion
for we are many.

He turns and signals the women to start. They start all together.

It's a while since you've been out.
You sit inside and
wait. Sometimes as if heard
or so you think. It seemed this way,
when you went outside and came
to the door.
Nothing. You live with it though.
Same every day

They stop, look at each other and round about

                        sometimes more so.
                 like voices somehow, more or less.
It is inside you.

That. Afterwards, though, comes the day
they come outside
you wait for them in the house.
Same day every time.
Sometimes in the morning when
you wake up it is as if you are stuck
and you prise yourself off them.
You want to stay a little more
you don't want to get up. You turn look
right left in case they came. No.
They haven't come. But get up
                        it's today.
Today. Get up.
Another year gone by and we will

They stop suddenly, for a few seconds, again, who is this?

be all together.
A few hours still. Then we will sleep,
wake up
will wait. Will sleep.
Wake up. Will wait.

All together. Narrator wipes his hands on his pullover,
signals to them, they stop, they would have continued.
He reads.

accounting that He
was able to raise them up

Smiling? As if he smiled. LG, with the cross, him also with
papers, reading from there. Bent over then leans on his el-
bow, as he reads he stretches out on his side.

bricks.
one more kick but then
you stop because you are in pain.
Wait a bit until it goes.
The whole arm going in. Opened.
It wasn't hard. Like that. Then
the mind stops for a little
stops

He stops, wonders

I remember
the last time. I left after that.
After some time I thought I heard something.

After that Him.
Every now and then He would come,
behind me all of a sudden. Telling me go.
She is there. Waiting for you.
I would turn my head.
Nothing. Then again. Then
every so often, many times it would not stop at all.
I wouldn't believe it. Then it was starting again. Like a
needle inside my ear
Here.

stutters

          and steps.
then nothing. I am sweating. I mop my brow
These hands are not mine, I don't feel
that

Stops, thinks about it. Starts again suddenly, as if in a hurry.

I put my head inside for a while, to see.
Hurts again. Wait a bit until it goes.
Sometimes you hear her clearly, now
the others cover her.
One on top of the other.
You hear her.
Like a wave inside you, all of a sudden.

Now I am above
I know she is there waiting for me
I hear her. She wants to come out.
A box and something moving inside it,
open it. Bones, earth. Close it.
Open it. Same again. You leave and
go back to it again. Why though.

I was coming and going. Seagulls.
Wouldn't leave me alone.
I found a cloth and wrapped it
around my feet because they were
swooping down
and pecking me. I got up again
to go. Going as far as I could.
Someone coughing
behind me, would stop start again,
but I wasn't turning around to see.
He stopped, finally.

He gets up to leave, Narrator signals to him, he sits down again, continues

I had found a blanket
to cover myself. I was sleeping outside.
Then I came and settled here.
It's a bit better here.

They might leave me alone.

Until now, every time I used to wake up,
every time

a towel on my face.
They were pouring in water on top.
I was drowning. They were taking it off.
Then I could I breathe for a while.
Then again. Then they would leave,
the others would come.

Night. Long shadow with an eye
behind it looking at me.
Shadows. More. Shorter and darker.
Digging. Stopping. Digging again
A little beyond

He holds the cross.

hammering on top and then
lowering them in. Somebody shouted.
What if they came this way.

The other signals him to stop, stops for a moment and then
continues

It hurts but I keep my mouth shut
because they might hear me.
Don't let it come out. Then they left and I slept
a bit. Silence. I hear her in there. She wants
to get out. Then again
silence.

Narrator, goes and stops him. Train, like a heart beating inside the bridge, we wait, it's gone, now the women, in their turn or nearly so.

A dog had come up outside the door.
Scratches and wants to come in
a little light in the window
but it is still early.   Out on the street
nobody yet. Let's go in and prepare. Fire.
They like it. But they will say nothing.
They will sit at the table
like always. They will eat huddled
over their plates, silent.
Last year he was holding a stone
some papers   he was wiping
his lips all the time   there was
something wrong with his lips
what is he saying

With the people from the bridge // 19

Water. Corn. And a little pomegranate.
They can't sit properly   the body is hard
doesn't soften. The arm-pits closed.
They can't hug you.
Eyes cast down. They will stand up and go
over there to that corner and will stay for a while and
then out in the garden and stand there,
at the same spot.
They will stand still, for a moment it is as if
they wanted to say something,
as if something rose in their throat,
but it's nothing.

It has boiled. A table-cloth. I will spread it myself.
Flour. Alright. Mix. A bit more.
Corn. Sugar. Alright. And some wine.
Turn on   turn on
Bring chairs. They will sit
where they used to

*Barking. Someone comes in, sits beside me. We go on, LG
down on his face now. Gets up puts his hand inside his trou-
sers, sits down again. Takes off one shoe.*

then I would hear footsteps again and

like somebody chewing.
Same thing every day.
This pain is like the clock that is heard
every time you pay attention to it.
Take it and throw it away.
The sun in a blur.
Closer to one eye than to the other.
You hear them above. They left again.
Silence.
Then again rain, no time to dry
the blanket. Then I went out
because I was hungry and
I went to find something to eat.
When I came back
they had put back the bricks
and had closed again.

Stops, carries on

hit harder and knock out the bricks.
Once you are in put them back in place.
Put back the blanket on top. Tear it a bit
for the light to come through.
I sat at your side
I knew you were there. Time passed.
As if I could see you. Half-opened mouth
eyes like then, in the end

Time passed.

I went out again and fetched some water.
A sip. Helps my stomach, it soothes me
and I can lie down for a little.
In sleep again, your voice coming strong.
I couldn't. I stood up
and was banging on the lid until it broke.
I took it out. I pulled her and turned her on her side.
I lifted her up. She fell again. Again.
Time passed.
In the end I got her out. I let her down and
went to see the blanket in case the wind
had blown it away. I went again and laid down
beside her. I was tired.
Enough light. A white worm, long.
A finger digging all by itself.
Leave something for me.
Something will be left in the end.
A tooth from her mouth.
something for me
a tooth

                                        broken

Takes the glass from the floor and drinks, leaves the pa-
pers, now by heart. My head aches since yesterday, today
no water at all, nor did I eat anything. After it's finished.
LG, continues

> Hairs stuck on her skin.
> She had sweated a lot.
> That smell beside me and
> I couldn't sleep.
> Then I slept a little. When I woke up
> I was holding her in my arms.
> Later, again I was searching for her in my sleep
> the way I used to back then. A hand
> that was drawing me in. Didn't know how.

Stops and starts again louder, pacing nervously up and
down, close to me something like laughter, but it was not.

> Earth had got into my eyes
> and they were smarting.
> Then I slept and was woken again
> by the dogs that had come and were
> barking on top
> I shouted to them.
> They were startled and fled and
> then I went back to sleep.

Narrator, interrupts him gives him another piece of paper
prompts him: they lie down then, LG carries on

Then. On their backs. In a line.
One to the side of the other.
They shut them in carefully
in case they went out.
Not quite. I pay attention
in case I hear someone.
No one.
What I hear has nothing to do with this.
There it is again. I heard it.
No, that's not it, it is them on top.
Someone shouted to somebody else
to go away from there. Same thing every time.
If they find me they will catch me and
won't let me go. They will take me away
to lock me up. The whole wall full of drawers.
They are about to open.
I went and pulled one.
And another one after that.
One under the other and to the side
and below. I close my eyes. You. In a haze.
Then I was again on top and
I was opening the hole again
just as He told me, don't stop He had told me.
I am not sure when this happened.

Opened. Here. She is just there.
She is waiting for you.
Dig and   you will find a door
underneath. And He told me she is in.
A tree growing downwards.
The others outside had lit a fire.
Tonight they have come, almost above us.
I saw them and sat still inside.

Us. In this room.
And those at our side and the others on top.
And us in between.
But you can't stay here for long
and there is nowhere to go.
Smoke coming in from above.
They will start to take them out again.
Eventually they will get
to us

they will separate us

He comes our way, they fill his glass, returns sits down and drinks. Comes and gives us to drink as well, I drank a little.

Now the women

Take a log and throw it on. I'll go down
and fetch some more so for them to dry.
They are hard to light because of the rain.
Went out again.
Wait. Soon they will come.
They will eat with us at
midday. Later the afternoon light
will stoop for a while
through the window.
When it gets dark they will leave,
and they will take something with them,
you don't really know what
but you will be missing something.
A log, you light it and it goes out again.
Together. When the light fails the walls rear up.
A hole as if the fire had opened it.
Bring some more wood.
Go down to the garden.
Some more wood.
A spider underneath that is waiting
to pounce on something. Pounces on it.
Pounced on it.
She will suck out
the inside. She wrapped it and left it

        to tug a little and goes
                            there as far as
        she knew
        You have understood. It grew dark
        for a moment. The rain got stronger and then
        it stopped altogether. You can't see,
        then you see again.
        Light again, same. The door
        opened closes closed yes
        open they came yes they come up the stairs

*The lights flicker for a while come on then it's all right. Seconds.
Then they flicker again and go out. Silence. Hum, now it
stopped. In the dark, for a while as if they had forgotten
about us, hum again, the lights return. Narrator with the
Bible.*

        for he saith; in a time accepted
        I have heard thee and in the day
        of salvation have I succoured thee;
        behold now is the accepted time
        behold now is the day of salvation

*Chorus. Burning newspapers. Narrator goes and turns on
the TV. Hum interference a shadow on the screen comes
and goes again. Woman, voice. At first only some words,
strained, then a little better, then the image a little more stable*

as well. NCTV. Then as if the screen split in two.

face down.
I couldn't.
Weight on my back.
I couldn't.
I wanted to turn.
Stone? On the back.
I couldn't get up.
Then it broke and opened.
Door. Air came in.
He held me. I was trembling.
I couldn't
the hands.
He couldn't lift me.
Heavy. It was heavy. Where was I.
They had forgotten me.

face down

Numbness. Pulled by
the shoulder and turned me
to the side. Then on my back. Bound
legs, bound
hands crossed on the chest.

Bound.
He tries to cut it.
Sheet.
Stuck to the mouth.
Cold. A rope
Hurts. Legs

Face on the screen, clearer, fairly clear, every so often the mouth opens but it is not heard or with a time lag. Gets bigger and for a few seconds very clearly. Right eye shut. The signal is lost again then again normal.

Then I sat upright for a while. Dizzy.
I couldn't close my mouth.
Open. I couldn't.
It was frozen. There was something inside
and he took it out. It had dried
and it hurt me.
He wiped my face with his hand.
Where was I. Who with.
I left or
they let me go. I left.
I got up. I see
       He is over me.
I am cold. Held me

and took me out.
Air

a hole in the breast

wheezing. Wait. Swelling out slowly.

Here it breaks up entirely, suddenly better again but not always that clear. Screen turns green.

I raised my arm a little. Slowly
with my fingers

I was searching –

mud in the mouth and a lot of
saliva. I spat.

Further inside

a piece from the sheet
in my teeth. A rag deep
in my throat all the way down.
He drew it out
and then with his tongue on my eye.
Then the other.
Sits beside me
and waits
for me to get up

something heard outside
I want to stand up
I reach for his hand

LG. Goes in front of the TV and stares at it. Her image and voice in sync. Sits down, his back to the wheel, his face under the screen, and then reads again from his papers. Their voices alternating, and for a while one overlaying the other, each in turn

She was face down inside. Why

Now I remember. Same as before

The body in two, the light on her belly

Same bed. Same room

No nails. One hand. On the other

Helped me to turn over. Cleaned me

Yes. And on the other hand the skin new.

Cover me

Palms wet. Held me by the shoulder

From my throat and he lifted me up

She can't sit upright. I laid down and waited

Lie down at my side

I will lie down

Here it is

Here. The bed. In front of the window

He continues alone, he has lain down

We are home. The way it used to be
then. Same light from the window.
Silent together.
Then she said something and
fell asleep again. That they had left her
alone for a while
but they will come back in the end.
Silent together in the dark. And the dog
as if crouched under the table.

No, it's not.

I feel the arms holding me now
I turn around to see you
your fingers take hold of my sides

squeeze   your mouth trembles

your body is warm.   your eyes

I don't know what they see.
A tiny hole in the lips. They tremble
and open   ants

Ants. Hesitates a little, cleans his mouth, continues

and saliva, sweat
something jabs from inside to get out,   ,a
                        the gauze around the hand
loosened
                        and then
                                        to
bend, down to the

From your arm-pits a trickle still runs
and drips down, dries sticks on your skin,
gelled, you are falling again.

And then she held me again.
Something deep in my throat.
Blocked. I can't breathe.
I hear my heart. I look
between your legs. A bulging
and a squeak. A mouse. One more.
Baby ones.

And again as if not even a day had passed
since. You get up
and hold me in your arms.
Then as if it were only
your voice. I held you
                    in the dark for a moment. Moon

the seagulls coming down above

Does not hear now. She slept again.
I had nothing
to cover her with
Cold. Froze again. As if she was here and
had left. Dark but something appears
at the window.
Get up and make a fire.

Turns a page, stops. It's cold. TV again. NCTV.

Cold sleep
a dream that
won't let you sleep long
Then it started to hurt me.
Not now, perhaps very slightly.
As if I was drowning and he pulled me out.
A wire bound around my hands,
the wood pressing on my breast.
Then I woke up again.
Lights a fire.

No image, just voice. My neighbours listen bent over. You are not in time, light does not help you, you hold on to whatever you can, not all. Leave it for later.

Didn't work. He turned and sat on the bed at my side. He looks for my hand. Laid down and hugged me. The others as if they had understood. They gathered and looked at us through the window. With my mouth on his chest. Still more. Were pushing the window but couldn't come in. They wanted to come with us. More outside the door and the door that was shuddering. Then somebody said: open up. Then they all said something together.

With the people from the bridge // 35

They were clinging onto the door and had climbed up. They were sitting on the door but couldn't get in. Don't open. Then nothing, looked like they had left, then again. If they could they would cry. Then again: open up. Don't open. I got up and sat upright on the bed. I was thirsty. A rope from above going down to the mattress. I was thirsty. Give me to drink. Lay down over me. You must drink if you want it to soften. We will stay here as much as we can. One arm feels a bit better, softer than the other. Dark and soft like liver. Come close. Put your legs like this. Hole. His body is warm. My hand in his hand. A hand coming from the other side. Inside my hand. Under his chest. You open your mouth and drink, you were so thirsty. You lay down at his side and he holds you again in his arms.

What I managed somehow like that, maybe even a bit better. The women go on burning newspapers, some don't take, smoke, they bring more, her face on the screen gets larger looks out towards   focus for a while on her nose. One nostril. One nostril. Then the hand. Wipes it. Continues

you are thirsty again. Very. All of a sudden. You drink again. The earth made you thirsty. Very.

A little bl

TV, voice clear. And as though in a hurry.

Time passed. I am sitting, beside him.
Listen how he breathes.
White tongue, mouth open
his wound has not yet dried
properly. I licked it. His head now.
I count hair by hair. Then he woke up
holds my head, kisses me, then again.
I count. I close my eyes.
I open them. Same thing again and again.
From the start, the same again.
Then again here.
All the same again like before,
you don't know how many times.

Time passed.
We are outside the house, at the door.
It was open.
We went up and sat side by side among them.
They had grown very old.
They were waiting around the fire and when
we went in they stood up.
I sat at his side. They stood up
and went inside all except one.

With the people from the bridge // 37

She had put her hands on his shoulders
and she was weeping. She was weeping.
She wouldn't stop.
Couldn't close her mouth.
Spit was dripping on him

*It stunk. Engine oil and rubber and smoke. Chorus. A cloth
wrapped around a stick, they soak it, throw it too into the
drum. They tore up two or three books too. Flames. All to-
gether, Chorus.*

How long have you been in. When was the last
time you went out. What is left for you is here.
You don't want to go out, you only remember
and wait, sit inside and listen to the rain.
You rake the ash.
 A half-burned twig curling upwards a little.
You stay inside. Wait.
Hush. Listen now. Did you hear?
They have come. They will sit side by side.
You will bring them something to drink.
This year they have come from farther away.
Let's sit all together.
Get up and come look through the window.
Look outside
They are coming, look at the street,
there are already enough of them

down there, look further back,
you see how many there are?
At the end of the street it is full. Wait a bit.
Do you see them there?
Like a wave that swells as it comes.
Full now. Here, look here.
A great flock splitting left and right.
Each one gets to his door
knows which one.
There is still something in their minds.
You wanted to go and find them.
But they come and find you before that.
Leave the door open for them to come in.
Listen. He is coming up the stairs.
Don't stand up. He is coming.
He came up. He has come.
They have come together.

Narrator. Has gone to the car and is checking something on the cassette-player. Two from the Chorus go and look in the car. Silent, still, begins again, NCTV. TV, clearly as before.

This is how it started. It was Him.
First time I saw Him. He told us to
come out, don't be afraid He told us
I will come back in the end

With the people from the bridge // 39

and take you with me.
I remember Him,
He was ushering us, each one of us
out of his door. Withered leaf
withered in the crowd.
A very strong wind forcing you forward.
Then in this room together with you
together like back then, then here with
them. Soon we will leave.

I remembered the staircase as soon as
I entered. I remembered
the time I had come here again,
from then to now
a lapse. Now you are sitting beside me.
Then I forget this as well
until I feel your hand.
I sit at your side and wait.
Soon we will leave. We will go back.
I can't see well.
I stretch out my hand I wanted to
talk but cannot
the others come in again
and now they sit around us
all together, staring at us.
It was as if they were afraid
to get close to us.

They wanted to give you to drink

              warm   black

I go closer

not red, black
and dries at once.
No time to drink
No time it's time to get up
you hold my hand and
we go down.

Narrator. Gets ready to read. Damp. I crouched a while on my knees. Put something underneath. Got up, two papers from where the women were bringing them. Sat down again.

Saturday. More today, two in front, the others in a pack and two at the end that had stopped and were staying behind. The one showed the other where it was. They went and waited for a while on top. Silence. Since yesterday someone had opened a hole and then covered it with a blanket pegged to the inside. They removed it, pulled out the bricks at the edge and made the opening larger. They went down. The one ahead pointed with his flashlight to the other: the lid was gone and she was laid out on her side. The other was bringing earth to the wall with the shovel for them to step on, when they would be ready to lift her up. Shovel. They dug underneath. It was stuck in the mud. First finish with that, then put her back in there and lift her up. Crowbar. Up and down, then further aside. Then with their hands, kneeling down. It was not coming up. It was stuck. He kicked it. He took the scarf off his face and wiped it. He put it back on. He dug with his foot below it a little and then used his hands. They lifted the one side up. Then they let it down again. They put her inside, face down. Inside there was someone else too. They dropped her on top of him. They put the lid back, forced it a little to close.

Saturday morning. The rest outside were bringing wood, brambles, whatever they found. Rain all night. Not so bad now. They threw on a torn piece from a tyre and a book. More rain. They sprinkled something on top from a bottle and threw in a match. Flames, then only smoke. They drenched a cloth and threw it in. Slowly, it took. Then a bag, they pulled out her shoes and her clothes and were throwing them on one by one waiting a while, clothes first, a shoe, a shoe. It nearly went out. They drenched another cloth. Yet another bag, yet other books. They were tearing, tearing, then on. And then the man with the shovel called the others to give them a hand to lift her up. They lifted it up. It was stinking and they didn't want to open it then and there. They went further off. The fire was good, and now it got stronger and stronger. It was today. Today was the day they were waiting for them. In the houses they had opened the doors and were waiting for them. What was it that was waking them up.

For they that are coming
declare plainly that they seek a country.
and truly if they had been mindful
of that country
from whence they came out,
they might have had opportunity
to have returned
and stayed there;
but now they desire a better country,
that is heavenly.
wherefore God is not ashamed
to be called their God;
for he hath prepared for them a city.

With the people from the bridge // 43

The lights flicker and go out. In the dark. The hum stopped.
Nothing yet. Then steps, still dark, silence. Some beside me
in low voices. Hum. The lights turn on, flicker, turn on. LG,
climbs in the car. Drags the iron sheet closed. Outside the
women whose low voices, whispering, are scarcely heard.
Chorus.

> Head bent over their plates
> almost hanging. Eat.
> And some wine. He reaches for the glass
> > spilt
> spilt on her hand. Let them
> go down to the garden, sometimes I thought
> I saw them under the laurel,
> a little further off.
> Two shadows. One. Two shadows.
> Then still for a while.
> Then they sit down. Then still again.
> Then she stretches out her hand.
> As if they remembered something to do.
> As if they are trying to understand something.
> And then this noise as always.
> And as if somebody
> told them to stand as if he woke them again.
> But they still want to stay a little more.
> They have lain down.

She has fallen on his chest.
They don't have much time.
They must leave soon.

Narrator. Turns on the cassette-player. LG, but not very clearly. Nod. He turns up the volume.

We went back.
They were around me again.
They spoke all together
I couldn't understand.
Then one by one. I still couldn't understand.
Then once more all together very fast.
They were stretching out
their hands and searching for me.
I didn't know where you were
I was going down below
                    a corridor downwards
stairs. I was feeling with my hands
on the wall
            like a face. I sat in a spot
took the blanket, covered myself,
my head too

With the people from the bridge // 45

I was hiding and waiting for you.
He came again.
I spoke to Him.
Don't torture me. I begged Him to help me.
He said he would come back and find us again.
He told the others to come out.
They were shouting to Him to let them
in somewhere else, wherever they could,
and my head was throbbing.
Before leaving He told me
turn back go home to your own.
I said I didn't have
I am cold

I am getting drowsy

                                        silence
I went down yet another

here,

                        I can't see in the dark
hand in front, one more step
ends, no going forward anymore
and then light from above, I could see.
Downstairs. Going down to the right.
Slowly now.

outside I hear the rain, here
it is better

                    as if breaking

                                  again
the seagulls. They have put their heads
inside

one more step. Water starts. I sit down.
Then I found you again. I sat at your side.
And they came out and
they went and entered somewhere else.
Could not hear them any more,
just the two of us now.
I held you in my arms.

Cassette-player stops, in the car a red light comes on. Narrator. Comes to us to read. Very close to us. He takes off his pullover and puts it on inside out. The women are burning incense? Comes from the oil drum.

There was a room and next to it one more, and another one beside that and another, and another, a city, but there were no streets there were no passages and there was no going from one place to the other, a hive they were digging and opening and closing from above. Warehouse and the boxes they were lowering in. Mouths open, opening and fed from above. They were closing, crumbling inside, opening, lowering again, opening closing crumbling opening only on top. A city you couldn't go anywhere. One would fall on the other and then they would go and bring more. And then they would wait for the mouths to empty. But the time would come and some of them would wake up below and search for an opening to get out and someone would hear them, someone or a dog and it would come and dig and get in and would open for them and they would get out, and a few had got out someone was saying and if we let them they will all get outside, and they will, and they will come and take us all there and no man will be left. And they were trying to find out at night nobody

slept somebody saw her when she came to take
him she took him with her she will take others too
hurry up we must go. Next morning they should
gather together to go and check if she is still in. Dig
and a few others to keep watch. But it's like, it's like
digging the sea and the more you dig the more you
upset them.

It had rained so much that all turned to mud. The
first ones they brought out were there as they had
left them days before. Yet warm if you touched
them, like eggs warm on your palm you could feel
something moving inside but only a little.

*Cassette-player, background noise, LG, his voice same as
before. Doesn't end in some places you will fill it in yourself*

I heard my name. You were gone but
you were here. Again. They called me. From
the door. Who is it I asked. They
told me come we will go together. I turned
and looked at you. Face down on
my chest. Them, a few yards
in front of me but I couldn't see them properly.
I stood up and went further in to see.
It wasn't a dream. My feet like in water.

I wanted to go deeper still
to make out who they were, I was going.
Couldn't see faces. I was asking but
all they would tell me was to go with them.
I put my hand on my chest
like a bite and the finger goes in.
No pain at all. The dog. As we went
it got still darker, in the distance appeared
the bridge. They were talking about me
I asked them what, don't talk, they said,
because He is everywhere, and He might
hear you. I wanted to go back, but
you had come to my side
and you were walking with me. I wanted to be
with you. You held my hand and
pulled me a little.
They turned and looked at us

Here almost nothing is heard. Something in the car, they are pulling and pushing, Narrator, turns it up louder. She bangs on the window, cries out, you can't hear what, presses her head to the glass. From the cassette-player.

Now He was passing over and coming towards us
from the bridge with the people
behind Him, all together.

50 // *With the people from the bridge*

They were following Him.
We were waiting on the opposite side.

Her inside and she continues to bang on the window. The
noise covers all and goes on a bit still, slowly it clears, her
own voice, probably, from the TV again,

he turned on his back. Opens his mouth.
He wanted to say something.
He fell again. Lifted his head a little.
He sees I am with him
and then falls, for a while holds me
by the throat
and then
empties   the flame
cleansed. We return together.
We will be there in a while.
Stay and rest a little.
On the way it was
dripping
a bit from his chest

he was tired
lie down
that he brought   up

It has not dried yet, still running.
There is still some, drips a little
from his chest.

                                    a little still
it will empty
You came. Now more than together.
They have come in, gather around you now. Flock
and with   more than
together. In a while you will be one
of the other parts,
mingled. We shall wait.
We shall wait for Him. When will He come
Smashed wood on the wave.
The heads will tilt up and will open
their eyes. Hands.
Slowly they will dry
and then He will come.

We arrived and we are waiting.
Their fire up there will not hold out for long.
They are getting ready here.
I hear them behind the
door   getting ready. They will come in
this way. They will join us.

                       on top and still digging.

Open up and see if there is anything.
They will bring out the body
but they won't find anything.

*Chorus, they go pull the rear door of the car, open and let
her out. I saw her leaving at the back in the dark. From
there it probably exits behind the bridge to the other side.
Behind me laughter, and a dog that doesn't stop. Narrator,
turns off the cassette-player. From the Book.*

They were not to be found
because God had translated them

*The women start with him, then stop, wait, start again
from the beginning*

They opened the door and went out.
The street is full again,
as long as there is light
you see them still leaving, you wanted to
hold them in your arms when they stood up
but you couldn't. Shadows that fall

one on top of the other. You look and see
them all coming together where the street ends.
Ended.
Papers burned and gone out.
There was a time we were
down in the garden together.
Do you remember with the dog?
Used to come, sit with us until evening,
then would go and come back the next morning.
Each one goes, one by one in their turn.
Until your turn comes.
Don't go out of the house.
If you are still here,
on a day like this they will come
again. Again.
The fire is not drawing, rake the ash a bit.
Take and fill a bag and leave it at the door.
Don't go out.

TV again, NCTV. Rain the same, perhaps even stronger, her
voice in between. Go out somewhere, eat and sleep.

Now it will open, you hear the hammer.
They will look at the mouth first.
It has drunk. Some fresh drops at the edge.
They will open the stomach and it will be full of it.
If they look further up

54 // With the people from the bridge

they will find two hearts. One smaller
and they drink from each other.

They won't go alone because they are afraid.
They go all together.
One of them opens the mouth and searches it.

Mud. Rain. Ash. Ground bones.
Grey dough. No worms at all.
The fire will not last long now.

Opened. The remainder wait for them
in the church.

*Train. Turns the cassette-player off. A few around me get up
and leave. Chorus, again. I listen, I don't care where it will end.*

Don't go out. Stay here until
they come and take you. If you go out
nobody will know you. Each one waiting
for their own, in a station
you don't recognize, a station inside
a church. I had a dream yesterday.
We were holding hands all together
around her and were looking at

the blood under her finger-nails.
And inside her lips.
And He came and took us by the hand
and we went down and out on to the street.
And at the end of the street there were
stairs and by way of the stairs you would go down
inside the church.
From there again you would go up.
And another staircase, and more
people and we all wanted to cross
to the other side.
You could see the water from up above.
Then we said we should lie down
one on top of the other
on top of the other. One on top of the other
until that fades too.
Don't go out.

*Something is happening in the car, one of the Chorus goes
from the back and pulls the door to open it. LG inside fallen,
they drag him, man-handle him, two by his legs two by his
arms, they are leaving quickly towards the back. NCTV, black
screen.*

They have woken up and are crawling
one on top of the other and in between
and they want to go out. But there is no exit,

not yet. They will wait.
It is raining and the rain comes
and softens the body,
and what was a burden to them
leaves them in their sleep. Last day, it is falling
you hear the sheet that has covered.
Covered. Covered.
Until He comes. When He comes He will
first strip out the earth above them
and He will give them to drink.
The house is rising
the people are waiting. One under the other.
What's left cannot be made out.
But after each one will take as is his.
And then as if this wave were breaking. Road.
Then it is the body again, arms lift up
legs walk, they go and find
their new clothes. They get dressed now.
We get dressed. Each one covers his pit.
They all hold each other and go up
one on top of the other
to reach and cling to the bridge. Across the way.
One on top of the other, they are
the bridge. One goes up on top of the other.
They step on and pass. Then the bridge fades.
They shout when they see that He is coming.
They run around Him. They cry.

With the people from the bridge // 57

You hold him in your arms.

Narrator, the only one left. He turns off the TV the lights come on. My two neighbors get up. Stopped raining now. Silence, nothing from the stage, alone, eyes fixed on the text.

They opened up finally and the others approached and saw them as they were laid inside together. Saturday. Between them a half-eaten blanket. Her on him, face down. Rain, very heavy. Someone went and brought a strap. They bound her and dragged her outside. Separated them. Rain, washing earth from her face and lips. They dragged her a few yards further off, he remained inside. A lot of water, and the body in the mud almost floating. A little earth on the lips. Mouth open, overflowing with rain water. The skin on one hand dry, new on the other. More gathered together. That dog again. Someone that went and threw lime in the pit but water was running inside and would fill it if they didn't act quickly. The moon was coming and had grown very big. Cries. Green stomach shining. Dark net of veins like a tree on her skin, lips almost black, a little blood on the chin. And the people will seek death and will not find it and they will try to die and death will escape them. Then the circle opened someone came through with a plank, sat on her with his legs astride. Her arms spread out above, plank, they bound them with wire on the plank and they were holding her tightly. Two were holding her arms. Bloated belly and stomach. Hammer, stake on the chest. It broke inside. Rattle. Blood. A lot. Fresh, first higher up then runs on her legs. Deflated. Wheezing. Time enough they waited for her to dry. One went in at the end with a bucket and baled out the water from the pit. Then back inside, and they fastened her with nails on it. They lowered her with the strap and a white cable. On the way down it was still dripping and perhaps it was not just from the rain. There may have still been more in her. They leave and tomorrow will come again to see if she has tried to get up and for a while they will still come to see if is open. They will wait. They will wait to see if it opens. Should she appear some place, her, somebody else, something they told you, something you heard behind your back. Don't look behind. They are ahead of you waiting.

He puts the book aside, comes to us and shares out the pages he was holding, whoever wants takes one, my neighbor leaves them and goes off and two more likewise. Why do I recall I took one and put it in my mouth. Paper like honey, sweet. Goes back again. With his back turned.

And set me down in the midst of the valley
which was full of bones
our bones are dried and our hope is lost
we are cut off; and he said unto me
son of man, can these bones live
and I answered, O Lord God, thou knowest.
and he said unto me, behold,
I will open your graves
and cause you to come up out of your graves
behold I will cause breath to enter into you
and I will lay sinews upon you
and will bring up flesh upon you
and will cover you with skin
and put breath in you
and ye shall live.